DISCARDED

MORRIS AUTOMATED INFORMATION NETWORK

0 1022 0445320 7

4/15

The Morristown & Morris Township Library
One Miller Rd.
Morristown, NJ 07960

THE BARNYARD

By CODY MCKINNEY

Illustrated by MAXINE LEE

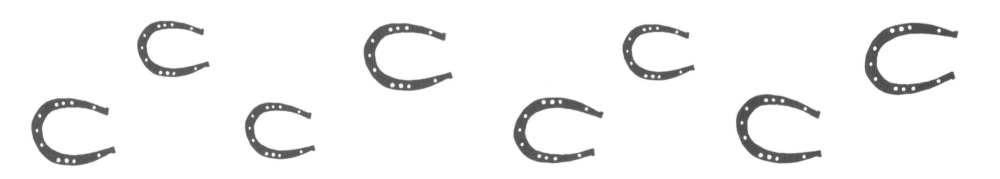

CANTATA
LEARNING
MANKATO, MINNESOTA

CANTATA
LEARNING
MANKATO, MINNESOTA

Published by Cantata Learning
1710 Roe Crest Drive
North Mankato, MN 56003
www.cantatalearning.com

Copyright © 2015 Cantata Learning

All rights reserved. No part of this publication may be reproduced
in any form without written permission from the publisher.

Library of Congress Control Number: 2014938326
ISBN: 978-1-63290-076-0

The Barnyard by Cody McKinney
Illustrated by Maxine Lee

Book design by Tim Palin Creative
Music produced by Wes Schuck
Audio recorded, mixed, and mastered at Two Fish Studios, Mankato, MN

Printed in the United States of America.

VISIT
WWW.CANTATALEARNING.COM/ACCESS-OUR-MUSIC

Barnyards are fun places to visit. They can also be a lot of work! There are many animals to take care of and **chores** to do. People who work at barnyards are very busy! What animals do you think live at a barnyard?

I wake up, and it's a sunny day.

I have to work, but it feels like play.

A rooster's cock-a-doodle-doo opens my eyes.

There's a calf, and he needs some grain.

I have to milk all the cows again.

They **graze** the **pasture** set beneath the skies.

The barnyard, where a foal is a baby horse.

The barnyard, for some food that we eat, it's the source.

On their **hooves** is how foals run and play.

If they need a snack, they can eat some hay.

And **domesticated** dogs run all around.

We work hard to grow veggies from the ground.

Down a road and just outside of town is a farm.

It has a barn and more land than I've ever seen.

The barnyard, it's where we get our milk and meat.

The barnyard, the chickens lay the eggs that we eat.

In the pens, we have our birds and pigs.

In the field, there are cows and sheep,

and the wool they let us have will keep you warm.

And at night, we all go to sleep.
We are tuckered out from the **mane** down to the feet.

We'll do it all again tomorrow **morn** . . . at the barnyard.

21

GLOSSARY

chore—a job that has to be done regularly

domesticated—tamed, no longer wild

graze—to eat grass that is growing in a field

hoof—the hard covering on an animal's foot

mane—long, thick hair that grows on the head and neck of some animals

morn—another word for morning

pasture—land where farm animals eat grass and exercise

The Barnyard

Cody McKinney

Pop Rock

Online music access and CDs available at www.cantatalearning.com

ACTIVITY QUESTIONS

1. Did you know a baby horse is called a foal? Did you know that a baby cow is called a calf? Can you think of other animals that are called different things when they are young?

2. Draw a picture of your favorite barnyard animal! What sounds does it make? Does it spend time with other barnyard animals?

TO LEARN MORE

Doyle, Sheri. *Cows*. Mankato, MN: Capstone Press, 2013.

Kuskowski, Alex. *A Flock of Sheep: Animal Groups on the Farm*. Minneapolis: ABDO Publishing, 2013.

Veitch, Catherine. *Farms Around the World*. Chicago: Heinemann Library, 2012.